Cover of the original manuscript, drawn by Woody Guthrie in 1948.

Woody Guthrie
with Marjorie Mazia Guthrie
Pictures by Woody Guthrie

HarperCollinsPublishers

NOTE FROM THE PUBLISHER

This book is a replication of an unpublished songbook, lost for over 40 years. It was written in the late 1940s by the legendary songwriter and folksinger Woody Guthrie and his wife, Marjorie Mazia, a modern dancer. Inspired by their own young daughter, the Guthries wrote these songs to perform and share with children.

Maintaining the integrity of the original *Woody's 20 Grow Big Songs*, a document which had long since become faded and dog-eared, was a labor of love for many people. Harold Leventhal at Woody Guthrie Publications, Inc. brought the book to us and provided continual guidance throughout the publishing process, as did Woody and Marjorie's family, especially their daughter, Nora Guthrie Rotante. Larry Richmond and Judy Bell at The Richmond Organization provided all of the accurate music and lyrics, and Christina Davidson painstakingly hand-lettered the first verses and music for each song.

From the original dedication to the timeless lyrics and music to Woody's own spirited artwork, the book remains as lively and vital today as it was the day Woody and Marjorie bound the original pages.

We hope *Woody's 20 Grow Big Songs* will find a special place in your home.

THIS BOOK IS DEDICATED

To the memory of Cathy Ann, whose words inspired it, whose playing gave birth to it, whose smile and whose laugh we try to catch parts of to make our hearts laugh, to make our books dance, today and tomorrow.

To Arlo Davy, just climbing up into your fourteenth month: You have played the mouth harp and danced now since you were twelve and a half months old, and have always been able to sing rings around me and stomp dance a circle around Marjorie. You'll give us all kinds of songs, games, jokes, joshings, dances, newer things to think and hope and to do in your new ways.

It is a book I took from Gwendolyn Gailer, from Susie Quewzer, from Mr. Squinty Bill, from watching Missy Tannywheeler, Miss Annie Banany, and Peter Jeeper & Suzie Warshoff, and from listening to Old Daddy Quist down in our cellar feeding his cats.

Marjorie wants this book to be a happy laugher and a goofy dancer, a high flinger, a bumpy jumper, a shy teaser, for all her kids already skipping, and for your kids' kids when they start hopping.

This book has come from all of you, and we hope it goes back again to where it comes from.

Cathy Ann Guthrie
Woody Guthrie
Marjorie Mazia Guthrie
Arlo Davy Guthrie
1948

WOODY'S 20

GROW BIG SONGS

no. 1 WAKE UP

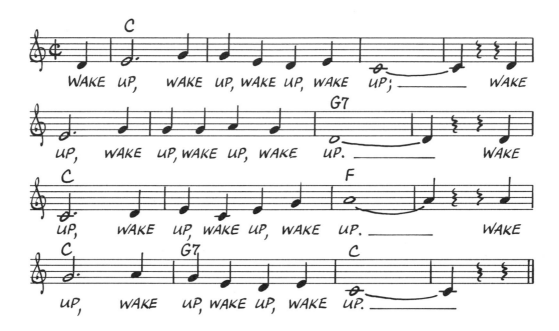

WAKE UP, WAKE UP, WAKE UP, WAKE UP; _____ WAKE
UP, WAKE UP, WAKE UP, WAKE UP. _____ WAKE
UP, WAKE UP, WAKE UP, WAKE UP. _____ WAKE
UP, WAKE UP, WAKE UP, WAKE UP. _____

Open eyes, open eyes, open eyes, open eyes;
Open eyes, open eyes, open eyes, open eyes.
Wake up, wake up, wake up, wake up.
Open eyes, open eyes, open eyes, open eyes.

Stretch arms, stretch arms, stretch arms, stretch arms;
Stretch arms, stretch arms, stretch arms, stretch arms.
Wake up, wake up, wake up, wake up.
Stretch arms, stretch arms, stretch arms, stretch arms.

Stretch feet, stretch feet, stretch feet, stretch feet;
Stretch feet, stretch feet, stretch feet, stretch feet.
Wake up, open eyes, and stretch your arms;
Stretch feet, stretch feet, stretch feet, stretch feet.

Stretch hands and toes and hands and toes,
And hands and toes and hands and toes.
Wake up and stretch your arms and feet;
Stretch hands and toes and hands and toes.

Wake up and play with all your toys.
Wake up, wake up, wake up, wake up,
And play with all the girls and boys;
Wake up, wake up, wake up, wake up.

Wake up, wake up, wake up, wake up;
Wake up and see the sun shine in,
And listen to all the things outside;
Wake up, wake up, wake up, wake up.

The fun of getting so nice and dirty
is to go and get cleano, cleano.

MA-MA, OH   MA-MA, _____ COME WASH MY FACE, _____

WASH MY FACE, ___ COME WASH MY FACE. ___ MA-MA, OH

MA-MA, _____ COME WASH MY FACE, _____

AND MAKE ME NICE _____ AND CLEAN-O. _____

number 2

Daddy, oh Daddy, come fix my shoe,
Fix my shoe, come fix my shoe.
Daddy, oh Daddy, come fix my shoe,
And polish it nice and cleano.

Sister, oh Sister, come bathe my back,
Bathe my back, come bathe my back.
Sister, oh Sister, come bathe my back,
And make it nice and cleano.

Cleano clean, yes, cleano clean,
Cleano clean, yes, cleano clean.
Scrubbity scrubbity and rubby-dub dubbity;
And make me nice and cleano.

Brother, oh Brother, come wash my hair,
Wash my hair, come wash my hair.
Brother, oh Brother, come wash my hair,
And make it nice and cleano.

Granny, oh Granny, come wash my feet,
Wash my feet, come wash my feet.
Granny, oh Granny, come wash my feet,
And make them nice and cleano.

Sweetie, oh Sweetie, come smell-a me now,
Smell of me now, come smell-a me now.
Sweetie, oh Sweetie, come smell-a me now,
Don't I smell nice and cleano?

3 MAILMAN

I SEE THE MAIL-MAN, MAIL-Y MAN, MAIL-ER MAN,

I SEE MIS-TER MAIL-ER MAN WALK-ING DOWN MY STREET.

Run, run, runny run, run,
Run, run, runny run, run
Run, run, run, and, run, run, run
I runny down the street.

Howdy, mister mailer man,
Howdy, mister mailer man,
Howdy, mister mailer man,
Have you a letter for me?

I will look and see, see,
I will look and see, see,
I will lookety look, see
If I've a letter for you.

Flippity, flippity, flip flap,
Flip flip, flipperty, flip flap,
Zipperty, zippy, zip, zoop zoop,
I'm looking in to see.

No, no, nizer, no, no,
No, no, nozeldy, no, no,
Bifferty, bofferty, boe, boe,
I have no letter for you.

Look, look, look again, please,
Look, look, look again, please.
Pleazeldy, weazeldy, cheezeldy, squeeze,
Look once more and see.

No, no, nizer, no, no,
Nope sir, nope sir, dear sir,
Snippers and snappers and rainbow clappers,
I see no letter for you.

Aww, gosh, aww, golly whillikinz,
Heck fire, gee, mister mailer man,
Aww, shuckers, jeeperz, creeperz,
Sniff, sniff, sniff, sniff, sniff.

Good-bye, mister maily man,
I guess I'll walk back home again.
I'll meet you here tomorrow
And ask you once again.

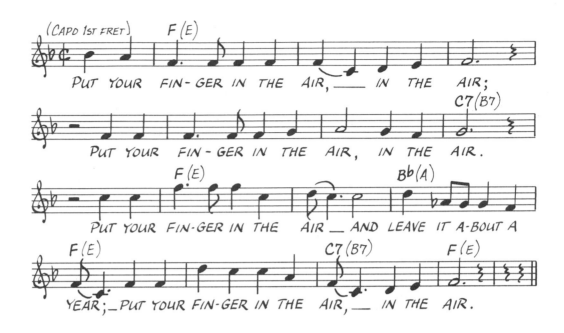

(CAPO 1ST FRET)   F (E)

PUT YOUR FIN-GER IN THE AIR, ___ IN THE AIR;

C7 (B7)

PUT YOUR FIN-GER IN THE AIR, IN THE AIR.

F (E)   Bb (A)

PUT YOUR FIN-GER IN THE AIR ___ AND LEAVE IT A-BOUT A

F (E)   C7 (B7)   F (E)

YEAR; __ PUT YOUR FIN-GER IN THE AIR, ___ IN THE AIR.

Put your finger on your head, on your head;
Put your finger on your head, on your head;
Put your finger on your head.
Tell me, is it green or red?
Put your finger on your head, on your head.

Put your finger on your nose, on your nose;
Put your finger on your nose, on your nose;
Put your finger on your nose
And feel the cold wind blow;
Put your finger on your nose, on your nose.

Put your finger on your shoe, on your shoe;
Put your finger on your shoe, on your shoe;
Put your finger on your shoe
And leave it a day or two;
Put your finger on your shoe, on your shoe.

no.
4

Put your finger on your chin, on your chin;
Put your finger on your chin, on your chin;
Put your finger on your chin—
That's where the food slips in;
Put your finger on your chin, on your chin.

Put your finger on your cheek, on your cheek;
Put your finger on your cheek, on your cheek;
Put your finger on your cheek
And leave it about a week;
Put your finger on your cheek, on your cheek.

Put your finger on your finger, on your finger;
Put your finger on your finger, on your finger;
Put your finger on your finger,
On your finger, on your finger;
Put your finger on your finger, on your finger.

Put your fingers all together, all together;
Put your fingers all together, all together;
Put your fingers all together
And we'll clap for better weather;
Put your fingers all together, all together.

Where do you want to put your finger next?
You sing it.

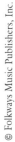

NO. **5**

Dance around

Hold up your hands,
Your hands, your hands,
Around and around and around.
Hold up your hands,
Your hands, your hands,
Around and around and around.

Walk on your toes,
Your toes, your toes,
Around and around and around.
Walk on your toes,
Your toes, your toes,
Around and around and around.

Now march and march
And march and march
Around and around and around.
Now march and march
And march and march
Around and around and around.

Now take big steps,
Big steps, big steps,
Around and around and around.
Hold up your hands
And take big steps,
Around and around and around.

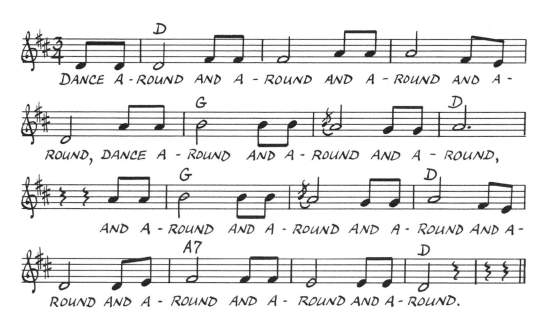

DANCE A - ROUND AND A - ROUND AND A - ROUND AND A -

ROUND, DANCE A - ROUND AND A - ROUND AND A - ROUND,

AND A - ROUND AND A - ROUND AND A - ROUND AND A -

ROUND AND A - ROUND AND A - ROUND AND A - ROUND.

Now it's time for you to make up your own words.
How about some like this?

Now hop like a bunny
like a bunny, like a bunny,
around and around and around.
And hoppity hop
like a bunny hops
around and around and around

You can run
runny run
like a horsie runs.
You can jump
jump jump
like a doggie jumps.

Now fly like a bird
like a birdie flies,
around and around and around…

See what I mean?
What do you want to dance around like?
Like a clown? Like a goofy man?
Like a lazy old turtle?
Like a what? What?

Okay, now you sing your own words, and all of us
will dance around like you tell us.

6 Don't You Push Me Down

(Capo 1st fret)

Chorus: F (E)

DON'T YOU PUSH ME, PUSH ME, PUSH ME,

Bb (A)   C7 (B7)

DON'T YOU PUSH ME DOWN. DON'T YOU PUSH ME,

F (E)

PUSH ME, PUSH ME, DON'T YOU PUSH ME DOWN.

VERSE: F (E)   Bb (A)

YOU CAN PLAY WITH ME. YOU CAN HOLD MY HAND.

C7 (B7)

WE CAN SKIP TO-GETH-ER DOWN TO THE PRET-ZEL

F (E)

MAN. YOU CAN WEAR MY MOM-MY'S SHOES, WEAR MY DAD-DY'S

Bb (A)   C7 (B7)

HAT. YOU CAN E-VEN LAUGH AT ME, _____

F (E)

_____ BUT DON'T YOU PUSH ME DOWN!

Grit your teeth,
Stamp your feet,
Look real tough,
Shake your finger.
Stick your chin out,
Feel real good and mad,
If you can feel mad and good at the same time!

(*Chorus*)

You can play with me.
We can build a house.
You can take my ball
And bounce it up and down.
You can take my skates
And ride them all around.
You can even get mad at me,
But don't you push me down.

(*Chorus*)

You can play with me.
We can play all day.
You can use my dishes
If you'll put them away.
You can feed me apples
And oranges and plums.
You can even wash my face,
But don't you push me down.

7

I like to walk with you on a day like this.
What is that pretty music I hear? Ohh, look…

(CAPO 1ST FRET)

F (E)   C7 (B7)

COME LET'S SEE THE MER-RY-GO-ROUND, THE MER-RY-GO-ROUND, THE

F (E)

MER-RY-GO-ROUND.   COME LET'S SEE THE MER-RY-GO-

C7 (B7)   F (E)

ROUND   GO ROUND AND A-ROUND AND A-ROUND. ___

Come, let's rub the pony's hair,
The pony's hair, the pony's hair.
There's lots of ponies that we can ride
Around and around and around.

Oh, now let's climb on the pony's back,
The pony's back, the pony's back.
Pick up the reins and buckle our straps,
Around and around and around.

It's off we go so nice and slow,
It's up to the clouds and down we go.
It's up and up, and down and around,
Around and around and around.

It's faster now the pony runs—
Up to the moon and down to the sun.
The pony runs to the music and drums,
Around and around and around.

Well, now he runs as fast as the wind,
He gallops, and trots, and dances a jig.
The pony is tired and he wants to slow down,
Around and around and around.

The pony stops and off I climb,
And off, and off, and off I climb.
I'll come back and ride you some other time,
Around and around and around.

8 JIG ALONG HOME

The fishing worm done the fishing reel.
Lobster danced on the peacock's tail.
Baboon danced with the rising moon.
Jig along, jig along, jig along home.
(*Chorus*)

And the rooster cut his weevily wheat.
The catfish tromped the cookoo's feet.
The ostrich stomped with the kangaroo.
Jig along, jig along, jig along home.
(*Chorus*)

VERSE:

WELL, I WENT TO THE DANCE AND THE AN-I-MALS COME, JAY-BIRD DANCED WITH HORSE-SHOES ON. GRASS-HOP-PER DANCED TILL HE FELL ON THE FLOOR. JIG-A-LONG, JIG-A-LONG, JIG-A-LONG HOME.

CHORUS:

G
JIG JIG-A JIG JIG-A

D7
JIG A-LONG HOME,

JIG JIG-A JIG JIG-A

C
JIG A-LONG HOME.

G7
JIG A-LONG, JIG A-LONG,

C
JIG A-LONG HOME,

G   D7
JIG JIG-A JIG JIG-A

G
JIG A-LONG   HOME.

And the mama rat took off her hat,
Shook the house with the old tomcat.
Alligator beat his tail on the drum.
Jig along, jig along, jig along home.
(*Chorus*)

The boards did rattle and the house did shake.
The clouds they laughed and the world did quake.
New moon rattled some silver spoons.
Jig along, jig along, jig along home.
(*Chorus*)

The nails flew loose and the boards broke down.
Everybody danced around and around.
The house come down and the crowd went home.
Jig along, jig along, jig along home.
(*Chorus*)

HOWDY DOO

Howdy do, Howdy do,
Howdy do, sir, doosie do,
Howdy do, oh, do, howdy do.
I will kiss you on your cheek,
I will shake you by the hand,
Howdy do, Howdy do, Howdy do.

CHORUS:

G   C
HOW-JI DOO-ZLE OO-DLE OO-JIE HOW-JA DO SIR DOO-BER

            D7   G
DOO-BIE HOW-JA DO SA-LOO-BER DOO-BIE HOW-JI-DO HOW-JI-

            C   D7   G
DO HOW-JI-HEE-JI-HI-JI - HO-JI HOW-JI - DO. _____

VERSE:

                G
YOU STICK OUT YOUR LIT-TLE HAND TO EV-'RY

C   D7
WO-MAN KID AND MAN AND YOU WAVE IT UP AND

                        G
DOWN ___ HOW-JI DO, HOW-JI DO. YES, YOU

C   D7   G
WAVE IT UP AND DOWN,___ HOW-JI DO. _____

9

When you walk in my door,
I will run across my floor,
And I'll shake you by the hand, howjido, howjido,
Yes, I'll shake it up and down, howjido.
(*Chorus*)

On my sidewalk on my street,
Any place that we do meet,
Then I'll shake you by your hand, howjido, howjido,
Yes, I'll shake it up and down, howjido.
(*Chorus*)

When I first jump out of bed,
Out my window goes my head,
And I shake it up and down, howjido, howjido,
I shake at all my windows, howjido.
(*Chorus*)

I feel glad when you feel good,
You brighten up my neighborhood,
Shakin' hands with ev'rybody, howjido, howjido,
Shakin' hands with ev'rybody, howjido.
(*Chorus*)

When I meet a dog or cat,
I will rubby rub his back,
Shakey, shakey, shakey paw, howjido, howjido,
Shaking hands with everybody, howdy do.
(*Chorus*)

ALL WORK TOGETHER

My sister told me,
Brother told me, too,
There's a lotsa work
That I can do.
I bring her candy.
Bring her gum.
But if we all work together
Hadn't oughtta take long.
(*Chorus*)

My daddy said,
And my grandpaw, too,
There's work, worka, work
For me to do.
I can paint my fence.
Mow my lawn.
But if we all work together,
It won't take very long.
(*Chorus*)

I tell Mom an' Daddy,
An' my grandpaw, too,
My sister an' my brother,
Lotsa work for me to do.
You can bring me pennies
And candy and gum;
But if we all work together
'Twon't take very long.
(*Chorus*)

Bling. Blang.
Hammer with my hammer.
Zingo. Zango.
Cutting with my saw.

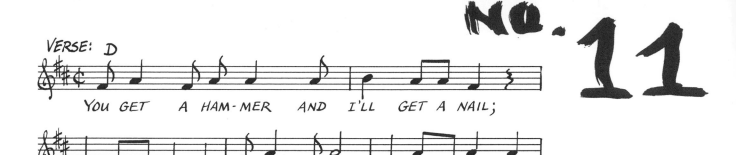

VERSE: D

You get a ham-mer and I'll get a nail;

You catch a bird and I'll catch a snail; You bring a board and

G

I'll bring a saw, and we'll build a house for the ba-by-o.

CHORUS: D

Bling blang, ham-mer with my ham-mer,

A7   G   D

Zing-o zang-o, cut-ting with my saw.

I'll grab some mud and you grab some clay
So when it rains it won't wash away.
We'll build a house that'll be so strong,
The winds will sing my baby a song.
(*Chorus*)

Run bring rocks and I'll bring bricks.
A nice pretty house we'll build and fix.
We'll jump inside when the cold wind blows
And kiss our pretty little baby-o.
(*Chorus*)

You bring a ladder and I'll get a box.
Build our house out of bricks and blocks.
When the snowbird flies and the honeybee comes,
We'll feed our baby on honey in the comb.
(*Chorus*)

needle SING

Who ever heard of a needle singing, anyhow?
I guess a needle could sing.
If you stitched it fast enough,
and knitted as fast as lightning,
and darned socks as fast as a whirlywind,
and sewed as fast as a racehorse.

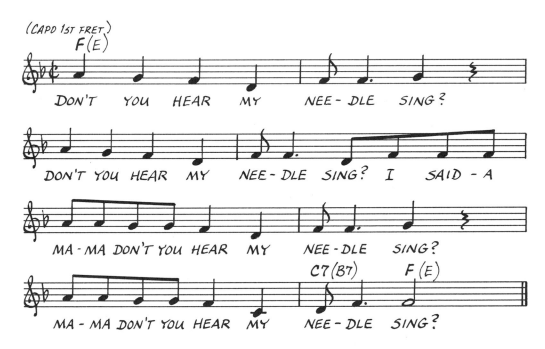

(CAPO 1ST FRET)
F (E)

DON'T YOU HEAR MY NEE-DLE SING?

DON'T YOU HEAR MY NEE-DLE SING? I SAID-A

MA-MA DON'T YOU HEAR MY NEE-DLE SING?

C7 (B7)   F (E)

MA-MA DON'T YOU HEAR MY NEE-DLE SING?

12

Chorus: Zinga zinga zinga zingy, needle sing.
Zinga singa singa singy, needle sing.
Zinga zinga zinga zingy, needle sing.
Mama, don't you hear my needle sing?

Knittin' for my daddy. Needle sing.
Knittin' for my daddy. Needle sing.
Knittin' for my daddy. Needle sing.
Mama, don't you hear my needle sing?
(*Chorus*)

Stitchin' for my brother. Needle sing.
Stitchin' for my brother. Needle sing.
Stitchin' for my brother. Needle sing.
Mama, don't you hear my needle sing?

Well, the baby ate the thimble. Needle sing.
The baby ate the thimble. Needle sing.
The baby ate the thimble. Needle sing.
Mama, don't you hear my needle sing?
(*Chorus*)

Oh, the kitten got my button. Needle sing.
Kitten got my button. Needle sing.
Kitten got my button. Needle sing.
Mama, don't you hear my needle sing?

Mama, don't you hear my needle sing? I sing-a
Mama, don't you hear my needle sing? I sing-a
Mama, don't you hear my needle sing?
Mama, don't you hear my needle sing?
(*Chorus*)

Oh, chicken in my basket. Needle sing.
Oh, chicken in my basket. Needle sing.
Oh, chicken in my basket. Needle sing.
Mama, don't you hear my needle sing?
(*Chorus*)

13 PICK IT UP

I drop my toys,
Pick 'em up, pick 'em up.
I drop my toys,
Pick 'em up, pick 'em up.
I drop my toys,
Pick 'em up, pick 'em up,
And put 'em back in their places.

I drop my candy,
Pick it up, pick it up.
I drop my candy,
Pick it up, pick it up.
I drop my candy,
Pick it up, pick it up,
And throw it away in the garbage.

I drop my apple,
Pick it up, pick it up.
I drop my apple,
Pick it up, pick it up.
I drop my apple,
Pick it up, pick it up,
And wash it clean in the water.

I drop my dolly,
Pick it up, pick it up.
I drop my dolly,
Pick it up, pick it up.
I drop my dolly,
Pick it up, pick it up,
And lay her back in her cradle.

I drop my shoe,
Pick it up, pick it up.
I drop my shoe,
Pick it up, pick it up.
I drop my shoe,
Pick it up, pick it up,
And put it with my other shoe.

I drop my head,
Pick it up, pick it up.
I drop my head,
Pick it up, pick it up.
I drop my head,
Pick it up, pick it up,
And put it back on my shoulders.

Pick pick pick it
Pick it up, pick it up.
Pick, pick, pick it,
Pick it up, pick it up.
Picka picka picky
Pick it up, pick it up,
Picka picka picka
Pick it up, pick it up.

(CAPO 1ST FRET) F(E)

I DROP MY THUMB, PICK IT UP, PICK IT UP. I

C7(B7)

DROP MY THUMB, PICK IT UP, PICK IT UP. I

F(E)

DROP MY THUMB, PICK IT UP, PICK IT UP, AND

C7(B7)   F(E)

PUT IT BACK WITH MY FIN — GERS.

What do you want to drop and pick up?
It's your turn, now.
Loud. *Louder.* I want to hear you.

14

It's too pretty to stay inside,
It's too windy to play outside,
So, what can we do with ourselves on a day like today?
Oh, yes, why didn't I think of it before?
If you'll promise to be real good,
and not kick all my paint off,
I'll take you riding in my car.

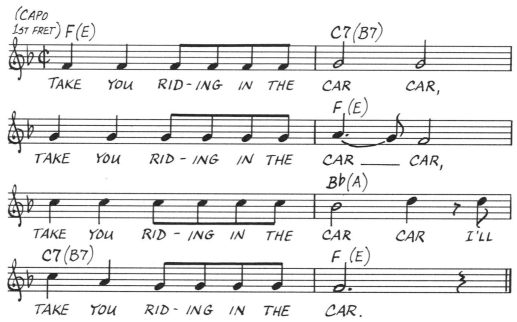

RIDING IN MY Car

(CAPO 1ST FRET) F(E)   C7(B7)

TAKE YOU RID-ING IN THE CAR CAR,

                                        F(E)

TAKE YOU RID-ING IN THE CAR _____ CAR,

                                Bb(A)

TAKE YOU RID-ING IN THE CAR CAR I'LL

C7(B7)   F(E)

TAKE YOU RID-ING IN THE CAR.

Click clack, open up the door, girls;
Click clack, open up the door, boys;
Front door, back door, clickety clack,
Take you riding in my car.

Climb, climb, rattle on the front seat;
Spree I spraddle on the backseat;
Turn my key, step on my starter,
Take you riding in my car.

Engine it goes brrm, brrm;
Engine it goes brrm, brrm;
Front seat, backseat, boys and girls,
Take you riding in my car.

Trees and the houses walk along;
Trees and the houses walk along;
Truck and a car and a garbage can,
Take you riding in my car.

Ships and the little boats chug along;
Ships and the little boats chug along;
Brrm brrm, brr brr brr brr brrm brrm
Take you riding in my car.

I'm a-gonna send you home again;
I'm a-gonna send you home again;
Brrm, brrm, brrm brrm, rolling home,
Take you riding in my car.

I'm a-gonna let you blow the horn;
I'm a-gonna let you blow the horn;
A-oorah, a-oorah, a-oogah, oogah,
I'll take you riding in my car.

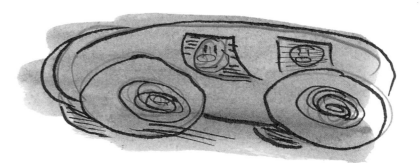

#15

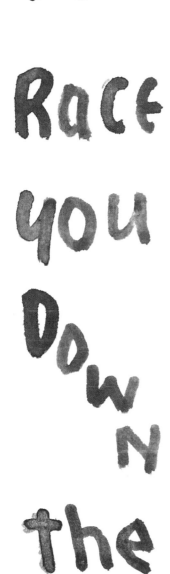

Race you down the

Mountain

I'll chase you round the bushes,
I'll chase you round the bushes,
I'll chase you round the bushes,
We'll see who gets there first.

Let's run and jump the river,
Let's run and jump the river,
Let's run and jump the river,
We'll see who gets there first.

I hear myself a-huffing,
A-huffing and a-puffing,
I hear myself a-huffing,
We'll see who gets there first.

Let's rest beside the water,
Let's rest beside the water,
Let's rest beside the water,
We'll see who gets there first.

Now,
I'll race you down the mountain,
I'll race you down the mountain,
I'll race you down the mountain,
We'll see who gets there first.

16... my dolly ...

My dolly walks for me, me,
My dolly talks for me, me,
My dolly walks and talks, and oh, she looks like this.
My dolly she can sing, sing,
My dolly she can dance, dance,
When dolly sings and dances, oh, she looks like this.
(*Chorus*)

Dolly says, I want to eat, eat,
Dolly says, I want to drink, drink,
When dolly eats and drinks, oh well, she looks like this.
Dolly plays with all the toys, toys,
She plays with girls and boys boys,
When dolly runs and skips, oh well, she looks like this.
(*Chorus*)

I know my dolly likes me,
And I know my dolly loves me,
When dolly hugs and kisses me, oh, we look like this.
My dolly's getting tired now,
My dolly wants to lie down,
When dolly goes to sleep, oh well, she looks like this.
(*Chorus*)

VERSE:

D

1. I PUT MY DOL-LY'S DRESS__ ON, I PUT MY DOL-LY'S
2. PUT MY DOL-LY'S STOCK-INGS ON, I PUT MY DOL-LY'S

PANTS ON, I PUT MY DOL-LY'S HAT ON, AND SHE
SHOES ON, SHE ACTS JUST LIKE A CLOWN-O', AND SHE

G   A7   1. D   2. D   CHORUS: D

LOOKS LIKE THIS. 2. I THIS. OH WELL, SHE LOOKS LIKE
LOOKS LIKE

A7   D

THIS, O.   OH WELL, SHE LOOKS LIKE THIS O.   TRA-

G   A7   D

LA-LA-LA-LA-LA-LO, AND SHE LOOKS LIKE THIS.

17 LITTLE Seed

VERSE:

TAKE MY LIT-TLE HOE___ DIG A HOLE IN THE GROUND.

TAKE MY LIT-TLE SEED___ AND I PLANT IT DOWN.

TOOK-Y TOOK-Y TOOK-Y TOOK-Y TI - DAL - O LET'S

ALL DANCE A - ROUND AND SEE MY LIT-TLE SEED GROW.

CHORUS:

TOOK-Y TOOK-Y TOOK-Y TOOK-Y TI - DAL - O

TOOK-Y TOOK-Y TOOK-Y TOOK-Y TI - DAL - O LET'S

ALL DANCE A - ROUND AND SEE MY LIT-TLE SEED GROW.

The rain it come
And it washed my ground.
I thought my little seed
Was going to drown.
I waded and I splashed
And I carried my seed.
I planted it again
On some higher ground.
(*Chorus*)

The sun got hot
And my ground got dry.
I thought my little seed
Would burn and die.
I carried some water
From a watering mill,
I said, Little Seed,
You can drink your fill.
(*Chorus*)

The snow it blowed
And the wind it blew;
My little seed,
It grew and it grew.
It grew up a cradle
All soft inside,
And a baby was sleeping
Covered over with vines.

[Woody never did get around to making up
music for this song.
The words are here; make up your own music!]

I'M A LIT-TLE BIRD YOU SEE SEE SEE, I

LIVE IN MY HOME IN MY NEST IN OUR TREE. MY

DAD-DY BRINGS MY MA-MA WORMS AND

MA-MA FEEDS THE WORMS TO ME.

Today my daddy flew out on our limb,
Didn't bring any worms to me all the day long.
He said, "Tweet, tweet, your day has come
To fly out from home and to catch your own worm."

My mother told me, "Your father is right.
You'll have to leave out of our nest and fly.
Your beak is full-grown, your wings, they are strong.
Today is your day to fly and catch your own worm."

"But Mommy, oh Mommy, you know I can't fly.
This wind is too cold, and our tree is too high.
I'm afraid to try to fly in the sky.
I'll fall, and I'll break my wing, and I'll cry."

Dad said, "You've got to fly out on your own,
To fly in the storm, and to fly toward the sun.
I'll peck, and I'll pecka you out of this nest—
I don't care a bit if you cry out your eyes."

It was pecky, peck, pecky, and picka pick pick,
They pecked me, they pushed me right out of our nest.
I fell through the sky till I learned how to fly.
I caught a big worm, and I never did cry.

Pretty and Shinyo

TAKE MY BRUSH, TAKE MY BROOM, CLEAN AND I CLEAN A-

ROUND MY ROOM, CLEAN AND I CLEAN A- ROUND MY ROOM TO

MAKE IT PRET-TY AND SHIN — Y - O.

19

Take my polish,
Take my cloth,
I rub and I rub
And I polish it off,
Rub and I rub
And I polish it off
To make it pretty and shinyo.

Take my soap,
Take my clothes,
Down and down
In the water they go,
Down and down
In the water they go
To make them pretty and shinyo.

Take my brush,
Brush my teeth,
Scrub 'em and I scrub 'em
And I brush my teeth.
Bubble and blow,
Bubble and blow
To keep them pretty and shinyo.

Tippy tappy toe
I go to bed,
Close my eyes,
And I rest my head.
Sleepy sleepy tight,
Sleepy sleepy tight
To make them pretty and shinyo.

I see a little sleepy eye.
Do you know whose eyes look sleepy to me?
Try to guess—
That's right. Yours.
Your eyes always come and tell me
when you are tired and sleepy, little sleep eye.

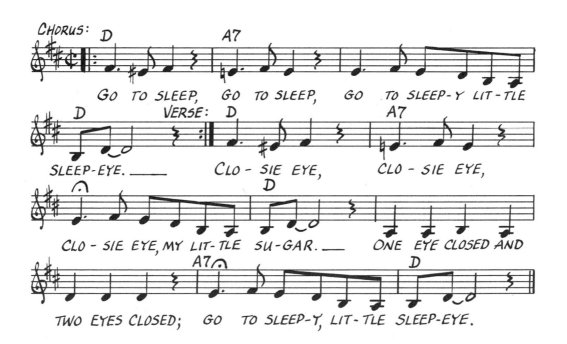

(*Chorus*)

Eyesie close, eyesie close,
Eyesie closed, my little sugar.
One hand asleep and two hands asleep,
Go to sleepy, little sleep eye.
(*Chorus*)

Dream a dream, dream a dream,
Dream a dream, my little sweeter.
Big dream, little dream, gotta go dream,
Go to sleepy, little sleep eye.
(*Chorus*)

Sleep, sleep, sleep, sleep,
Sleepy, sleepy, little sleep eye.
Sleep, sleep, sleep, sleep, sleep, sleep, sleep,
Sleepy, sleepy, little sleep eye.

Woody's 20 Grow Big Songs
Copyright © 1992 by Woody Guthrie Publications, Inc.

All rights reserved. No part of this book may be used or reproduced in any manner whatsoever without written permission except in the case of brief quotations embodied in critical articles and reviews. Printed in the United States of America. For information address HarperCollins Children's Books, a division of HarperCollins Publishers, 10 East 53rd Street, New York, NY 10022.

Typography by Al Cetta
1 2 3 4 5 6 7 8 9 10
First Edition

Library of Congress Cataloging-in-Publication Data
Guthrie, Woody, 1912–1967.
 [Songs. Selections]
 Woody's 20 grow big songs : songs and pictures / by Woody Guthrie, with Marjorie Mazia Guthrie.
 p. of music.
 Summary: An illustrated collection of songs, accompanied by their musical arrangements.
 Unacc. melodies; includes chord symbols.
 ISBN 0-06-020282-3. — ISBN 0-06-020283-1 (lib. bdg.)
 1. Children's songs. [1. Songs.] I. Guthrie, Marjorie, ill.
II. Title. III. Title: 20 grow big songs. IV. Title: Twenty grow big songs. V. Title: Grow big songs.
M1997.G98W6 1992   91-753710
                                                         CIP
                                                         M AC